THIS TRAVEL JOURNAL

BELONGS TO:

_____

_____

DREAMER.

PLANNER.

ADVENTURER.

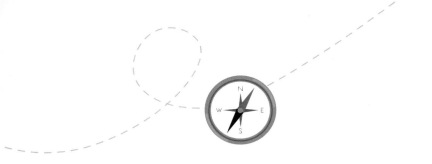

YOU MAKE KNOWN TO ME THE
PATH OF LIFE;
YOU WILL FILL ME WITH JOY IN
YOUR PRESENCE.

PSALM 16:11

All Scripture quotations are taken from the Holy Bible, New International Version®, NIV®.
Copyright © 1973, 1978, 1984, 2011 by Biblica, Inc.® Used by permission.
All rights reserved worldwide.

Cover and interior design by Studio Gearbox

Dream, Plan, and Go Adventure Journal
Copyright 2020 Text © Rachel McMillan. Artwork © Laura L. Bean
Published by Harvest House Publishers
Eugene, Oregon 97408
www.harvesthousepublishers.com

ISBN 978-0-7369-7971-9 (pbk)

Printed in China

HARVEST HOUSE PUBLISHERS
EUGENE, OREGON

20 21 22 23 24 25 26 27 28 / RDS / 10 9 8 7 6 5 4 3 2 1

Contents

Take the Leap

*The purpose of life is to live it, to taste experience
to the utmost, to reach out eagerly and without fear
for newer and richer experience.*

ELEANOR ROOSEVELT

*M*y hope is that you'll keep this journal as a souvenir and snapshot of your bravery in travel. Yes, bravery! Whether that bravery manifests in teaching English overseas for a year or in taking a day trip to discover a new city in your own state, record your adventures and times of self-discovery right here. And let me tell you a secret: When you become confident enough to venture outside of your comfort zone in one facet of your life, that confidence trickles into other areas as well.

In this journal, jot down both your big escapades and smaller forays—anytime you venture to a new place of any kind. That's whether you patronize an out-of-the-way coffee shop that's the perfect setting to finish the novel you're reading (or writing!) or you visit an exotic garden by adding a day to a work trip. Or, if you're like me, whether you take yourself on a honeymoon to Vienna!

In my late twenties, after years of dreaming about that gorgeous Baroque city as the ideal honeymoon destination, I considered what would happen if I never married. Would I never go to Vienna? I couldn't live with that idea, so off I went—alone. That first Vienna trip later inspired my writing the book *Dream, Plan, and Go* to encourage women to step forward in their journeys, whether solo or with others. Either way, we women get to know ourselves a little better when we dare to leap toward the newer and richer experience. This journal will encourage you to take that leap, in your own way and for your own reasons.

Adventure always: Continually watch for opportunities to take excursions, detours, and leaps toward new experiences. Adventure awaits not just tomorrow or a year from now but in the present. So why *not* now? This travel journey will keep that pursuit alive.

Adventure intentionally: Make plans with intention. Small steps or big leaps, they all matter. This journal will help you notice who you're becoming and celebrate the bravery and joy you find as you taste those experiences fully. There's space for notes from ten trips and room to dream.

Adventure thoughtfully: Notice who you are and what you love. Think about what matters to you. This journal prompts you with tips and pages to preserve your plans and capture your thoughts, sensations, and discoveries. If you need inspiration as you write on the entry or blank pages, turn to the Journaling Jump-Starts on page 152 to get the ideas flowing.

One day you'll look at these written snapshots of when you took leaps and explored new places. When you stepped out of your comfort zone. When you watched a dream become a plan that shaped an experience, creating memories to relish! It will all be here in the pages of your adventure.

My Trip Wish List

Create a wish list of places you'd like to go.

Destinations might be two towns over or an ocean away!

Where:

Why:

When: ...... Now ...... Soon ...... Someday

Where:

Why:

When: ...... Now ...... Soon ...... Someday

Where:

Why:

When: ...... Now ...... Soon ...... Someday

Where:

Why:

When: ...... Now ...... Soon ...... Someday

Where:

Why:

When: ...... Now ...... Soon ...... Someday

Where: ....
Why: ....

When: ...... Now ...... Soon ...... Someday

Where: ....
Why: ....

When: ...... Now ...... Soon ...... Someday

Where: ....
Why: ....

When: ...... Now ...... Soon ...... Someday

Where: ....
Why: ....

When: ...... Now ...... Soon ...... Someday

Where: ....
Why: ....

When: ...... Now ...... Soon ...... Someday

Adventure Chart

Consider these types of adventures when making your plans.

The Inspired Adventure is born of a lifelong desire to experience a place.

The Urban Adventure takes you into the heart of a bustling metropolis.

The Backyard Adventure prompts you to explore your neighborhood, town, city.

The Formative Adventure introduces you to your strengths and preferences.

The Spiritual Adventure leads you to a retreat, pilgrimage, or anything that feeds the soul.

The Unplanned Adventure beckons you to say yes to short-notice travel such as a side excursion on a work trip or a journey inspired by a great airline ticket price.

The Sensory Adventure heightens all five senses and immerses you in something new.

The Purposeful Adventure is taken with the intention to serve, teach, help others in some way.

The Daring Adventure ushers you outside of your comfort zone.

On My Way To:

....

....

dream

Where I want to go: _____

_____

Why I want to go here: _____

_____

_____

_____

_____

_____

What inspired the idea of this adventure: _____

_____

_____

_____

_____

_____

_____

_____

_____

_____

_____

plan

Possible dates:

Travel companions or trip contacts
(people who are resources or who you will visit):

Research and website references:

Transportation info:

What I want to see and do:

People I am with or have met today:

Today's travelogue:

Today's highlight:

People I am with or have met today:

Today's travelogue:

The view from where I sit right now:

People I am with or have met today:

Today's travelogue:

What I want to remember about the people I've met:

People I am with or have met today:

Today's travelogue:

How I feel in this moment:

People I am with or have met today: _____
_____
_____

Today's travelogue: _____
_____
_____
_____
_____
_____
_____
_____
_____
_____
_____
_____
_____

What I ate recently: _____
_____
_____
_____
_____

People I am with or have met today:

Today's travelogue:

One thing I want to remember about myself:

People I am with or have met today: _____

_____

_____

Today's travelogue: _____

_____

_____

_____

_____

_____

_____

_____

_____

_____

_____

_____

_____

An experience that challenged or inspired my faith and courage:

_____

_____

_____

_____

People I am with or have met today: _____

_____

_____

Today's travelogue: _____

_____

_____

_____

_____

_____

_____

_____

_____

_____

_____

_____

A gift of this adventure so far: _____

_____

_____

_____

_____

Financial Planning for a Trip

Even planning your travel budget can build anticipation. While you think through possible costs, you're also looking up places to stay or reading guidebooks or talking to others who've been to the place you want to visit.

As you make a budget, consider the following:

- Transportation for getting to your destination: air, bus, or train fare; car rental; gas for your car

- Metro passes, cabs, rideshares, and any other transportation you'll need during the trip

- Meals per day, plus beverages and snacks

- Ticket prices and entrance fees for plays, concerts, movies, museums, and other fun outings

- Safe and convenient accommodations

Savvy Sojourning Tip

If you want to visit a European holiday market but find the flights at Christmas too expensive: consider looking into those that open in November and check out cities that host Easter markets as well.

My Dream
Awaits In:

....

COMPOSITION
BOOK

dream

Where I want to go: _____

Why I want to go here: _____

_____

_____

_____

_____

When I picture myself here, I feel: _____

_____

_____

_____

_____

_____

_____

_____

plan

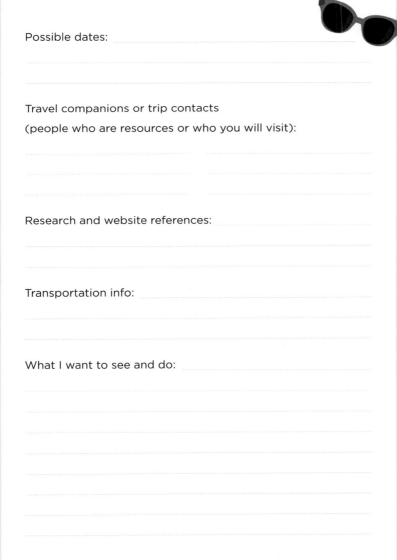

Possible dates:

Travel companions or trip contacts
(people who are resources or who you will visit):

Research and website references:

Transportation info:

What I want to see and do:

People I am with or have met today:

Today's travelogue:

Today's highlight:

People I am with or have met today:

Today's travelogue:

The view from where I sit right now:

People I am with or have met today:

_____

_____

Today's travelogue:

_____

_____

_____

_____

_____

_____

_____

_____

_____

What I want to remember about the people I've met:

_____

_____

_____

_____

People I am with or have met today: _____

_____

_____

Today's travelogue: _____

_____

_____

_____

_____

_____

_____

_____

_____

_____

_____

_____

How I feel in this moment: _____

_____

_____

_____

_____

People I am with or have met today: _____
_____
_____

Today's travelogue: _____
_____
_____
_____
_____
_____
_____
_____
_____
_____
_____
_____
_____

What I ate recently: _____
_____
_____
_____
_____
_____

People I am with or have met today:

Today's travelogue:

One thing I want to remember about myself:

People I am with or have met today:

Today's travelogue:

An experience that challenged or inspired my faith and courage:

People I am with or have met today:

_____

_____

Today's travelogue:

_____

_____

_____

_____

_____

_____

_____

_____

_____

_____

_____

A gift of this adventure so far:

_____

_____

_____

_____

_____

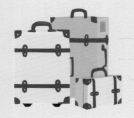

Essentials to Pack

When packing, think ahead to what you'll truly need and want most, and then leave the other stuff at home. Here are some ideas:

- Take clothing with interchangeable colors and patterns.
- If you'll be walking a lot, pack flats, sneakers, and a pair of ankle boots or other stylish choice in case you go to a nice restaurant or show.
- Include scarves and sweaters for layering.
- Pack international chargers (if needed) and one extra phone charger.
- Take an external battery case that extends the life of your phone or other tech items.
- Bring several sizes of plastic zip bags for wet items or lotions or to create handy compartments.
- Take a week's extra supply of medications. Travel with prescription medications in the original bottles just in case. If you travel internationally, check embassy websites for any medication requirements, such as a note from your doctor.
- Don't forget items you're used to having at home, such as: tape, sewing kit with scissors (ensure scissors are in a checked bag), feminine hygiene products, emery board, extra pairs of contact lenses or backup eyeglasses.

Savvy Sojourning Tip

*L*ine your luggage with gently-scented softening sheets or a lavender pouch. It can make clothes that have been sitting in a suitcase for a long time smell fresh.

I've Packed
My Bags For:

....

dream

Where I want to go:

Why I want to go here:

This trip makes my bucket list because:

plan

Possible dates:

Travel companions or trip contacts
(people who are resources or who you will visit):

Research and website references:

Transportation info:

What I want to see and do:

People I am with or have met today:

Today's travelogue:

Today's highlight:

People I am with or have met today:

Today's travelogue:

The view from where I sit right now:

People I am with or have met today:

Today's travelogue:

What I want to remember about the people I've met:

People I am with or have met today:

Today's travelogue:

How I feel in this moment:

People I am with or have met today:

Today's travelogue:

What I ate recently:

People I am with or have met today: _____

_____

_____

Today's travelogue: _____

_____

_____

_____

_____

_____

_____

_____

_____

_____

_____

_____

_____

One thing I want to remember about myself: _____

_____

_____

_____

_____

People I am with or have met today:

Today's travelogue:

An experience that challenged or inspired my faith and courage:

People I am with or have met today: _____

_____

_____

Today's travelogue: _____

_____

_____

_____

_____

_____

_____

_____

_____

_____

_____

_____

_____

A gift of this adventure so far: _____

_____

_____

_____

_____

Air Travel Tips

Consider these down-to-earth suggestions before you soar.

- For peace of mind, add an extra hour to the suggested time to arrive at an airport.
- Study an airport's terminal maps online before you arrive, especially if you have a transferring flight. Then you can ensure you know the fastest way to your next gate.
- If you can, schedule your flight to arrive during daylight hours. Stepping into a new-to-you place when it's dark can be disorienting.
- If you're overwhelmed when you arrive at your destination, stop at a Starbucks in the airport or check in with home to give yourself time to adapt to a new place.
- Don't book a tour, event, or performance for the day you arrive. You'll need time to adjust to a new culture and settle in.

Savvy Sojourning Tip

Entrust a family member or friend with a copy of your passport and your entire travel itinerary. Include flight and hotel details.

So Begins My
Adventure In:

dream

Where I want to go:

Why I want to go here:

Three things I hope to gain from this trip are:

plan

Possible dates:

Travel companions or trip contacts
(people who are resources or who you will visit):

Research and website references:

Transportation info:

What I want to see and do:

People I am with or have met today:

Today's travelogue:

Today's highlight:

People I am with or have met today: _____

_____

_____

Today's travelogue: _____

_____

_____

_____

_____

_____

_____

_____

_____

_____

_____

_____

_____

_____

The view from where I sit right now: _____

_____

_____

_____

_____

_____

People I am with or have met today:

Today's travelogue:

What I want to remember about the people I've met:

People I am with or have met today:

Today's travelogue:

How I feel in this moment:

People I am with or have met today:

Today's travelogue:

What I ate recently:

People I am with or have met today:

_____

_____

_____

Today's travelogue:

_____

_____

_____

_____

_____

_____

_____

_____

_____

_____

_____

_____

_____

One thing I want to remember about myself:

_____

_____

_____

_____

_____

People I am with or have met today:

Today's travelogue:

An experience that challenged or inspired my faith and courage:

People I am with or have met today:

Today's travelogue:

A gift of this adventure so far:

Foodie's Travel Plan

Are you someone who searches for restaurants weeks in advance of your trip? Here are some ways to get your foodie fix:

- If you're fond of a particular food or meal, try it at various restaurants and keep track of your reviews.
- Read reviews of restaurants in advance and choose a couple of places you hope to sample in each place you visit. And ask a local foodie to suggest a place you haven't read about!
- Consider an accommodation with a refrigerator and microwave in the room and a market nearby so you can enjoy restaurant leftovers and shop for go-to snacks.
- Hotel websites often offer a breakfast buffet that a travel site might not feature. Check for the best deals as you budget for your trip.
- Ask other travelers and hotel personnel for restaurant suggestions so you can balance an adventurous palate with staying healthy in a foreign country.

Budget for one nice restaurant in a new city. Take advantage of street food and buffet breakfasts built into hotel stays to save toward a splurge on a nicer meal.

Finally,
I'm Traveling To:

....

....

dream

Where I want to go:

Why I want to go here:

This trip is well-timed because:

plan

Possible dates:

Travel companions or trip contacts
(people who are resources or who you will visit):

Research and website references:

Transportation info:

What I want to see and do:

People I am with or have met today:

Today's travelogue:

Today's highlight:

People I am with or have met today:

Today's travelogue:

The view from where I sit right now:

People I am with or have met today: _____

_____

_____

Today's travelogue: _____

_____

_____

_____

_____

_____

_____

_____

_____

_____

_____

_____

_____

What I want to remember about the people I've met: _____

_____

_____

_____

_____

_____

People I am with or have met today: _____

_____

_____

Today's travelogue: _____

_____

_____

_____

_____

_____

_____

_____

_____

_____

_____

_____

How I feel in this moment: _____

_____

_____

_____

_____

People I am with or have met today: _____
_____
_____

Today's travelogue: _____
_____
_____
_____
_____
_____
_____
_____
_____
_____
_____
_____

What I ate recently: _____
_____
_____
_____
_____

People I am with or have met today: _____
_____
_____

Today's travelogue: _____
_____
_____
_____
_____
_____
_____
_____
_____
_____
_____
_____
_____

One thing I want to remember about myself: _____
_____
_____
_____
_____

People I am with or have met today:

Today's travelogue:

An experience that challenged or inspired my faith and courage:

People I am with or have met today:

Today's travelogue:

A gift of this adventure so far:

L ove the local cuisine? Buy a cookbook as your souvenir. Or order one online to have waiting for you at home and buy regional spices to take back. Be sure any food-related items can go through customs.

You Can Be Your Own Best Company

You can learn so much when you celebrate your own company. You'll be empowered in situations you manage alone, and you'll find inspiration in times of reflection.

Here are some ideas to get you out and about on your own at home or on a trip:

- Choose something you love to do and make a concerted effort to plan for it—perhaps in celebration of your birthday.
- Block off a day and time on your calendar and stick to it.
- Prepare and plan with the same care and devotion you would give to a date with another person.
- Take your book or your journal as your companion.
- If a meal is part of your date, don't think you have to rush through it.

Savvy Sojourning Tip

Make that date with yourself right now. Choose an activity you usually do with a plus one. Go to a movie. Attend an event. Linger over lunch at a café while enjoying your company.

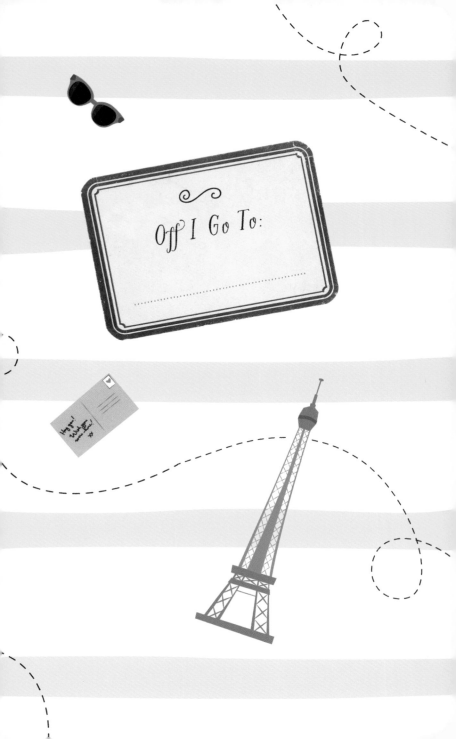

Off I Go To:

dream

Where I want to go: ....

Why I want to go here: ....

....

....

....

....

Something I hope to discover about myself on this trip is: ....

....

....

....

....

....

....

....

....

plan

Possible dates:

Travel companions or trip contacts
(people who are resources or who you will visit):

Research and website references:

Transportation info:

What I want to see and do:

People I am with or have met today:

Today's travelogue:

Today's highlight:

People I am with or have met today: _____

Today's travelogue: _____

The view from where I sit right now: _____

People I am with or have met today:

Today's travelogue:

What I want to remember about the people I've met:

People I am with or have met today: _____

_____

_____

Today's travelogue: _____

_____

_____

_____

_____

_____

_____

_____

_____

_____

_____

_____

How I feel in this moment: _____

_____

_____

_____

_____

People I am with or have met today:

Today's travelogue:

What I ate recently:

People I am with or have met today: _____

Today's travelogue: _____

One thing I want to remember about myself: _____

People I am with or have met today:

Today's travelogue:

An experience that challenged or inspired my faith and courage:

People I am with or have met today:

Today's travelogue:

A gift of this adventure so far:

Style and Self

One joy of traveling is discovering more about ourselves. But don't leave behind who you already know you are and want to be when it comes to your style.

- If you wear makeup, simplify your style with one favorite color palette for eyeshadow, blush, and lipstick.
- Pack clothing items that suit your look and complement your travel clothes.
- It's safer to act like a resident and not a tourist. Dress the part in comfortable clothes that allow you to move easily and give you confidence.
- Accessories like scarves in favorite colors dress up a tunic with tights for an evening out while still allowing you to shine as you.
- Consider buying a nice style piece as a souvenir that you'll use and treasure. Perhaps a scarf, bracelet, charm, purse, or special pen to chronicle your adventures.

Savvy Sojourning Tip

Is there a statement piece of jewelry, a favorite top or kind of makeup that you save for special occasions because they make you feel your best? Honor your dream by wearing it on your trip. (Mine is red lipstick!)

I'm Taking the
Leap To:

....

dream

Where I want to go: _____

_____

Why I want to go here: _____

_____

_____

_____

_____

_____

One souvenir I would love to find and buy on this trip is: _____

_____

_____

_____

_____

_____

_____

_____

_____

_____

plan

Possible dates:

Travel companions or trip contacts
(people who are resources or who you will visit):

Research and website references:

Transportation info:

What I want to see and do:

People I am with or have met today: _____
_____
_____

Today's travelogue: _____
_____
_____
_____
_____
_____
_____
_____
_____
_____
_____
_____

Today's highlight: _____
_____
_____
_____
_____

People I am with or have met today: _____

_____

_____

Today's travelogue: _____

_____

_____

_____

_____

_____

_____

_____

_____

_____

_____

_____

The view from where I sit right now: _____

_____

_____

_____

_____

People I am with or have met today: _____
_____
_____

Today's travelogue: _____
_____
_____
_____
_____
_____
_____
_____
_____
_____
_____
_____

What I want to remember about the people I've met: _____
_____
_____
_____
_____
_____

People I am with or have met today:

_____

_____

Today's travelogue:

_____

_____

_____

_____

_____

_____

_____

_____

_____

_____

_____

_____

_____

adventure awaits

How I feel in this moment:

_____

_____

_____

_____

People I am with or have met today:

Today's travelogue:

What I ate recently:

People I am with or have met today: _____

_____

_____

Today's travelogue: _____

_____

_____

_____

_____

_____

_____

_____

_____

_____

_____

_____

One thing I want to remember about myself: _____

_____

_____

_____

_____

People I am with or have met today:

_____

_____

_____

Today's travelogue:

_____

_____

_____

_____

_____

_____

_____

_____

_____

_____

_____

_____

An experience that challenged or inspired my faith and courage:

_____

_____

_____

_____

People I am with or have met today:

_____

_____

Today's travelogue:

_____

_____

_____

_____

_____

_____

_____

_____

_____

_____

_____

_____

A gift of this adventure so far:

_____

_____

_____

_____

How to Be a Respectful Traveler

A key word for the adventuress is *humility*. This is particularly important when you travel internationally. Look at life through the viewpoint of someone who makes their home there.

- Do research in advance about expectations for how a woman dresses and interacts with others.
- Pay attention to what is appropriate. Innocent words and hand signals in North America may have a different meaning elsewhere.
- Don't go to a new place expecting to teach; rather, go expecting to learn.
- Seek out the centers many towns offer for visitors to get a firsthand account of their culture and their religious views.
- Find a safe, private online space to ask questions rather than using a public forum like Instagram or Twitter. Also, many places have photography and social media laws you'll need to adhere to.

Savvy Sojourning Tip

Show respect by learning a few local phrases and branching out with local activities and cuisine. Most residents will appreciate the effort.

Excited for
My Trip To:

....

dream

Where I want to go:

Why I want to go here:

In this setting, I hope to experience:

plan

Possible dates: ....
....
....

Travel companions or trip contacts
(people who are resources or who you will visit):

....
....
....

Research and website references: ....
....
....

Transportation info: ....
....
....

What I want to see and do: ....
....
....
....
....
....
....
....

People I am with or have met today: _____

_____

_____

Today's travelogue: _____

_____

_____

_____

_____

_____

_____

_____

_____

_____

_____

_____

Today's highlight: _____

_____

_____

_____

People I am with or have met today: _____

Today's travelogue: _____

The view from where I sit right now: _____

People I am with or have met today:

Today's travelogue:

What I want to remember about the people I've met:

People I am with or have met today:

Today's travelogue:

How I feel in this moment:

People I am with or have met today:

Today's travelogue:

What I ate recently:

People I am with or have met today:

Today's travelogue:

One thing I want to remember about myself:

People I am with or have met today: _____

_____

_____

Today's travelogue: _____

_____

_____

_____

_____

_____

_____

_____

_____

_____

_____

An experience that challenged or inspired my faith and courage:

_____

_____

_____

_____

People I am with or have met today:

_____

_____

_____

Today's travelogue:

_____

_____

_____

_____

_____

_____

_____

_____

_____

_____

_____

_____

_____

A gift of this adventure so far:

_____

_____

_____

_____

Making Friends Along the Way

In Hollywood, the phrase "meet cute" refers to the humorous and unexpected moment in film when the hero and heroine connect for the first time. But making connections with other people as you travel need not be romantic moments that lead to a woman upending her life after a whirlwind connection with a man in a foreign place! Chances are, the personal treasures of your trip will be when you have a conversation with a local at an outdoor cafe, or share a transit ride with someone, or walk with another tourist on a group tour around a garden. Sometimes you find the courage to talk to a stranger or practice a foreign language with a comfort you might not feel at home.

Sometimes, if we are truly fortunate, we find a connection with a place and with a human being at the same time.

Savvy Sojourning Tip

Stay open. The person on the train who asks to borrow your phone charger might be the one who introduces you to the ideal spot to visit in the next town.

Ciao!
I'm Leaving For:

....

dream

Where I want to go: ....

....

Why I want to go here: ....

....

....

....

....

....

The dream and possibility of this trip inspires me right now

because: ....

....

....

....

....

....

....

....

....

plan

Possible dates: _____

_____

_____

Travel companions or trip contacts
(people who are resources or who you will visit):

_____   _____

_____   _____

_____

Research and website references: _____

_____

_____

Transportation info: _____

_____

_____

What I want to see and do: _____

_____

_____

_____

_____

_____

_____

People I am with or have met today:

_____

_____

Today's travelogue:

_____

_____

_____

_____

_____

_____

_____

_____

_____

_____

_____

Today's highlight:

_____

_____

_____

_____

People I am with or have met today:

_____

_____

_____

Today's travelogue:

_____

_____

_____

_____

_____

_____

_____

_____

_____

_____

The view from where I sit right now:

_____

_____

_____

_____

People I am with or have met today:

Today's travelogue:

What I want to remember about the people I've met:

People I am with or have met today:

_____

_____

_____

Today's travelogue:

_____

_____

_____

_____

_____

_____

_____

_____

_____

_____

_____

_____

_____

How I feel in this moment:

_____

_____

_____

_____

_____

People I am with or have met today:

Today's travelogue:

What I ate recently:

People I am with or have met today: _____

_____

_____

Today's travelogue: _____

_____

_____

_____

_____

_____

_____

_____

_____

_____

_____

_____

One thing I want to remember about myself: _____

_____

_____

_____

_____

People I am with or have met today: _____
_____
_____

Today's travelogue: _____
_____
_____
_____
_____
_____
_____
_____
_____
_____
_____
_____

An experience that challenged or inspired my faith and courage:
_____
_____
_____
_____
_____

People I am with or have met today: _____

_____

_____

Today's travelogue: _____

_____

_____

_____

_____

_____

_____

_____

_____

_____

_____

_____

_____

A gift of this adventure so far: _____

_____

_____

_____

_____

All Trips Can Be Romantic

The word *romance* doesn't always refer to love. It also refers to the eighteenth-century movement in art and literature. To be a romantic was to adhere to the poetry, intellectual thought, philosophy, literature, and art forms that exposed emotion, passion, and focus on the individual experience.

Romanticism can include the celebration of:

- nature
- beauty
- imagination
- inspiration
- intuition

Which of your interests align with romanticism? You deserve to look at life romantically. Whether at home or on a trip, turn your mind toward the rewards of romantic travel. Your understanding of and appreciation for beauty will expand.

Savvy Sojourning Tip

Embrace your romantic side. Sign up for a dance or art class. Go to a museum. Take a nature walk. Beauty and possibility are everywhere.

Can't Wait to
Get To:

....

dream

Where I want to go: ....
....

Why I want to go here: ....
....
....
....
....
....

This trip makes my bucket list because: ....
....
....
....
....
....
....
....
....
....

admit one

plan

Possible dates: _____

adventure awaits

Travel companions or trip contacts

(people who are resources or who you will visit):

_____

_____

Research and website references: _____

_____

Transportation info: _____

_____

What I want to see and do: _____

_____

_____

_____

_____

_____

People I am with or have met today:

Today's travelogue:

Today's highlight:

People I am with or have met today: _____
_____
_____

Today's travelogue: _____
_____
_____
_____
_____
_____
_____
_____
_____
_____
_____
_____

The view from where I sit right now: _____
_____
_____
_____
_____

People I am with or have met today: _____

_____

_____

Today's travelogue: _____

_____

_____

_____

_____

_____

_____

_____

_____

_____

What I want to remember about the people I've met: _____

_____

_____

_____

_____

People I am with or have met today:

Today's travelogue:

How I feel in this moment:

People I am with or have met today: _____

_____

_____

Today's travelogue: _____

_____

_____

_____

_____

_____

_____

_____

_____

_____

_____

_____

What I ate recently: _____

_____

_____

_____

_____

_____

People I am with or have met today: _____
_____
_____

Today's travelogue: _____
_____
_____
_____
_____
_____
_____
_____
_____
_____
_____
_____

One thing I want to remember about myself: _____
_____
_____
_____
_____

People I am with or have met today: _____
_____
_____

Today's travelogue: _____
_____
_____
_____
_____
_____
_____
_____
_____
_____
_____
_____
_____

An experience that challenged or inspired my faith and courage:
_____
_____
_____
_____

People I am with or have met today: _____
_____
_____

Today's travelogue: _____
_____
_____
_____
_____
_____
_____
_____
_____
_____
_____
_____

A gift of this adventure so far: _____
_____
_____
_____
_____

Reflect and Rejoice

Once your laundry and unpacking are done and you've settled back into your daily routine, find ways to savor the experience you had.

- Visit a local restaurant that serves the cuisine you enjoyed on your trip, and then set apart a time for reflection.
- Read back over this journal to remember some of your favorite moments.
- Go through your photos and select ones to print and frame, ones to post, and a couple to place on the photo pages in this journal. But why stop there? Scrapbook your boarding pass, a few favorite ticket stubs or train tickets, or even your metro card.
- Invite a couple of friends over to look at photos with you or to hear some of your highlight stories as you share a recipe or treat from the region you visited.

Whether you traveled with others or alone, list the following:

One thing I learned: _____

_____

_____

_____

_____

One thing I want to teach someone else:

One thing I wanted to try but didn't:

One expectation that wasn't reality:

One challenge I overcame:

One moment for which I am grateful:

Where to Next?

*U*se this space to write down specific dreams as they come to you, making a list of three possible adventures for each of five categories. Invite friends to help you brainstorm. Maybe some travel plans will emerge right then and there.

Backyard Adventure (discover a place where you live or in a close city or town):

1.
2.
3.

Daring Adventure (push beyond your comfort zone):

1.
2.
3.

Purposeful Adventure (go do good in the world!):

1.
2.
3.

Inspired Adventure (which places call to you?):

1.
2.
3.

Sensory Adventure (what trips will awaken your senses?):

1.
2.
3.

What about your previous journeys has inspired or guided the ideas you've listed?

JOURNALING JUMP STARTS

If you're sitting at a table or on a park bench with your journal open and your pen ready, but you aren't sure what to record, the prompts on these pages will jump start your reflections.

❑ What encouragements can you give yourself about your decision to dream, plan, and go?

❑ What interests or hobbies do you most enjoy solo? What about with others?

❑ What do you prefer when it comes to activities, pace of travel, food tastes, or accommodations?

❑ Which of your strengths helped you say yes to this adventure?

❑ When have you stepped beyond your comfort zone and experienced an empowering moment?

❑ What aspect of nature is evident and engaging in your current setting?

❑ How are you inspired by your experience? Is there an inspiring aspect of this trip that could also be incorporated into your life at home?

❑ What are the high and low points of this adventure?

❑ What has surprised you most about yourself? What has surprised you most about this location?

❑ Which friend would most enjoy the same outing?

❑ Explain why you are likely to make small talk, encourage deep conversation, or keep to yourself when seated next to someone you don't know.

❑ What have you have tried, done, or seen that's given you a boost of confidence?

❑ What are the top three things you like about a city? A rural, wooded, or coastal setting?

adventure awaits

❑ Describe a standout moment in detail so that when you're home you won't forget the mood or order of events.

❑ What have you learned about yourself and travel? What will you do differently on your next trip?

❑ Let your senses lead the way to record what will become treasured memories later. Write about what you've encountered in each of the sense categories.
Sight / Sound / Taste / Scent / Touch

❑ What did I pack that I either didn't use or could have done without?

❑ What did I not pack that would have been helpful?

my go-to packing list

- ☐
- ☐
- ☐
- ☐
- ☐
- ☐
- ☐
- ☐
- ☐
- ☐
- ☐
- ☐
- ☐
- ☐
- ☐
- ☐
- ☐
- ☐
- ☐
- ☐
- ☐
- ☐
- ☐
- ☐
- ☐
- ☐
- ☐
- ☐

my go-to packing list

- ❑
- ❑
- ❑
- ❑
- ❑
- ❑
- ❑
- ❑
- ❑
- ❑
- ❑
- ❑
- ❑
- ❑
- ❑
- ❑
- ❑
- ❑
- ❑
- ❑
- ❑
- ❑
- ❑
- ❑
- ❑
- ❑
- ❑
- ❑
- ❑

addresses

Friends at Home and New Friends Met Along the Way

Name:

Address:

Phone: Email:

Other info:

Name:

Address:

Phone: Email:

Other info:

Name:

Address:

Phone: Email:

Other info:

Name:

Address:

Phone: Email:

Other info:

Name:

Address:

Phone: Email:

Other info:

Name:

Address:

Phone: Email:

Other info:

Name:

Address:

Phone: Email:

Other info:

Name:

Address:

Phone: Email:

Other info:

Name:

Address:

Phone: Email:

Other info:

Name:

Address:

Phone: Email:

Other info:

Name:

Address:

Phone: Email:

Other info:

Name:

Address:

Phone: Email:

Other info:

Name:

Address:

Phone: Email:

Other info:

Name:

Address:

Phone: Email:

Other info:

personal and emergency details

Name:

Address:

Phone number:

Email address:

Emergency contact:

Known allergies or medical conditions:

Medical insurance/doctor information:

Additional details:

RACHEL McMILLAN

dream
plan
& go

a travel guide to inspire your independent adventure

ARTWORK *by* LAURA BEAN

Don't wait for adventure to come to you—go find it!

Get the confidence you need to embrace new experiences both home and abroad with this companion travel guide from savvy sojourner Rachel McMillan.

From pastries in Vienna to becoming a tourist in your own town, Rachel has great ideas to share for excursions both big and small and helpful tips to keep you safe, organized, and on budget while traveling solo.

You deserve the chance to discover the joy of being your own best company—this book will show you how!